THE MENTOR'S GUIDE

THE MENTOR'S GUIDE

Fostering Meaningful Educational Relationships

AVERY NIGHTINGALE

Creative Quill Press

CONTENTS

1	Introduction	1
2	Understanding the Role of a Mentor	3
3	Building Trust and Rapport	5
4	Effective Communication Strategies	7
5	Setting Goals and Expectations	9
6	Providing Guidance and Support	11
7	Nurturing Personal and Professional Growth	13
8	Addressing Challenges and Obstacles	15
9	Celebrating Successes and Milestones	17
10	Evaluating and Reflecting on the Mentorship	19
11	Creating a Lasting Impact	21
12	Conclusion	22

Copyright © 2024 by Avery Nightingale

All rights reserved. No part of this book may be reproduced in any manner whatsoever without written permission except in the case of brief quotations embodied in critical articles and reviews.

First Printing, 2024

CHAPTER 1

Introduction

Stating that this book serves as a guide is misleading; rather, it is a manual for building one-on-one relationships with colleagues in higher education that are aimed at learning and growth. It addresses the personal, idiosyncratic, messy reality of learning how to mentor. The book is based on a simple yet solidly established concept: the impetus for learning to be a mentor comes from practice guided by reflection on the practice and from learning in a community of colleagues. The author carries this concept through the book, providing abundant practice and suggestions for reflection. Each chapter ends with detailed exercises designed to help prospective mentors understand their concerns, beliefs, and assumptions about learning and teaching and the ways in which these influence their relationships with proteges. The exercises instruct mentors how to test and possibly change these beliefs and assumptions and how to draw on them to foster protege learning and development. This book will be especially helpful to new mentors who are considering their relational stance in the face of ambiguous and often conflicting advice on how to mentor. In these nine chapters, we will explore the meaning of developmental mentorship, to learn what to do with proteges in complex and uncertain situations that do not match up with script-like understandings of teaching, learning, and development. The author presents a definition of mentorship and a typology of mentor roles. As with any learning, learning to be a mentor is most effective when it occurs through engagement with others. So, the book will be very useful to those involved in mentor development programs or in forming communities of mentors in fields of higher education and K-16 teaching.

CHAPTER 2

Understanding the Role of a Mentor

A mentor is an experienced and trusted friend, usually attached to the lived experience of the individual midwife. This definition brings a general understanding of a mentor, but it is important for midwives to explore the concept in more depth. Cohen (2000) has suggested that people can use the word mentor to mean anything from a critical friend to a life coach. Barriball and While insert "Mentors might be seen as tutors, assessors, professional role models, confidantes, and are part of a supportive network." These perspectives all identify varying aspects of the mentor role. NMC standards are in place to ensure that all new practitioners will have the opportunity to work with a mentor who has undertaken a preparatory programme. The interest here is in the quality of mentoring that provides the best learning experience for students. Succeeding in doing so will ensure the health of the profession, as new recruits are nurtured and supported to become productive and satisfied workers. The meaning a mentor has come to know and understand has significant implications for both the mentor and the student who is seeking to learn. Understanding the student as a unique individual who is the sum of their part experiences directs the mentor to facilitate their learning in a way that is tailored to the student's needs. The belief that adult learners are self-directed and that learning is a mutual and reciprocal process, relevant to both the mentor and the student, has implications for the mentor in promoting the student's own initiative for learning and maximizing the opportunities in which the two can learn together from real practice situations. The NMC states that in order to meet your requirements as a mentor, you will need to demonstrate your ability to meet outcomes, but how do mentors meet these outcomes? These outcomes refer to the evaluation of nursing and midwifery students during their courses. Mentors will enable students to allocate 40% of their time in practice to acquire the required outcomes and overall course in order to be declared on the registrants' parts of the NMC standards. pp/s 7.

CHAPTER 3

Building Trust and Rapport

Be a good listener. Listening is the cornerstone to all interpersonal relationships, and is a skill that must be continuously developed. It is difficult for most of us to listen to others without thinking about how it relates to us, or without thinking of advice we want to offer. One should also not confuse hearing with listening; simply being in the presence of a mentee does not mean that effective listening is taking place. For most people, 90% of what they learn comes from what they say, not what the other person says. The mentor who is a good listener helps the mentee feel cared for and valued. This is all to the benefit of the relationship.

Be consistent. Inconsistency will sabotage even the best intentions. If mentors work with their mentees as their schedules permit, they will find that mentoring never happens. A regular time like every Tuesday after school or the first Saturday of the month will increase commitment and foster dependability.

Be dependable. A trusted mentor is reliable. If you say you will meet with the mentee at three o'clock on Friday, make every effort to do so. It is also important for the mentor and the mentee to start and end their meetings on time. This does not mean that time constraints never alter the meeting schedule, but it is essential for the mentee's sense of worth and security to know that the mentor values meeting with them.

CHAPTER 4

Effective Communication Strategies

An effective communicator will also present their message in a manner that is easy to understand. Using short, simple sentences is the best way to do this. This makes it easier for the receiver to take in what is being said. It is also a good idea to ask the receiver to repeat what has been said. This ensures that they have understood the message.

When sending a verbal message, it is always a good idea to be as direct and clear as possible. People have a habit of leaving out information because they believe it to be irrelevant. More often than not, though, it is this "irrelevant" information that gives the receiver a full understanding of what the speaker is trying to say. A simple example would be this: Dave asks John, "What time does Sue get in?" John replies, "The same time she did yesterday." Now, this may seem like a clear and concise answer to John, but for Dave, who was not present when Sue arrived the day before, this is not enough information.

Since the beginning of time, people have been communicating with others. Whether it be through body language, written communication, or verbal communication, getting your message across is a very important key to success. However, when communicating with other people, it can be easy for one party to misunderstand the other. We call this noise. Noise can affect any type of communication. It can change the meaning of a message, prevent a message from being understood, or it can stop a message from being sent or received. This is why it is so important to know the most effective communication strategies. This chapter will mainly focus on verbal communication and part of non-verbal communication. Note that gender, culture, and age should all be considered throughout each of these strategies. This is because the same message can be interpreted differently depending on these factors. A good communicator knows how to get their message across to all kinds of people.

CHAPTER 5

Setting Goals and Expectations

Once goals have been defined, the next step is to set expectations. The mentor needs to constantly monitor their expectations of the protege and be aware of when it is time to adjust them. Unrealistic expectations can lead to frustration, disappointment, and negative attitudes toward a once successful relationship. The protege should also express any preconceived notions or myths they may hold about the mentor role. This sort of thought pattern can become a barrier in their relationship if it is not openly discussed. Both parties may also reveal personal concerns or fears they have that could affect their investment in the relationship. By identifying these issues early on, solutions and preventions can be put in place to avoid adverse effects on the relationship.

Setting goals and expectations involves collaborative discussion and planning between the mentor and protege. It is during the goal-setting phase that the relationship begins to form and hardships may occur. It is important for both parties to take the time to consider what they want to gain from the partnership and what it will take to get there. It is imperative that the mentor guide the protege into creating short and long-term goals that are attainable yet challenging, relevant to their needs and desires, and providing direction for the relationship. This can be difficult for the mentor as they try to teach the protege goal-setting and planning skills without directly doing it for them. If the protege has no idea what they want to gain from the relationship, the mentor can provide a sample list of possible goals for them to review and further tailor to their liking.

CHAPTER 6

Providing Guidance and Support

The mentor can also help their protege better understand themselves. This can be accomplished through applying various assessment tools to clarify strengths, weaknesses, interests, and values. The mentor can then help the protege set long and short-term goals and develop plans to achieve those goals based on the results of these assessments. Through academic advising, the mentor can help the protege relate what the protege has learned about themselves to a choice of a major and a future career.

When offering guidance, the mentor should help a protege understand the university culture. The mentor can do this by helping the protege build relationships with faculty and staff, explaining policies and procedures within departments and the university, sharing strategies for academic success, and clarifying the rationale behind specific courses. Understanding the culture will help the protege take full advantage of what the university has to offer.

One of the major responsibilities of a mentor involves providing guidance and support to their protege. This role requires effective communication and the ability to listen to the concerns of your protege. The mentor should possess an understanding and helpful attitude, and mentors should provide career and academic guidance to their protege as well.

CHAPTER 7

Nurturing Personal and Professional Growth

To provide opportunities for protégés to build new skills and knowledge or refine existing ones, mentors can engage protégés in thoughtful analysis of their teaching, research, or other scholarly work. At times, reflection may involve a critical incident in which the protégé has done something to produce an unexpected and undesired outcome. In such cases, mentors can help by asking questions that stimulate reflection, without pushing the protégé to become defensive about the situation.

Effective mentors seek to understand where a protégé is in his or her career and then help provide experiences that are developmentally appropriate for moving to the next level. Issues of career balance, the development of the professional self, and identity transformation are all part of the professional growth and development process. By creating experiences that are challenging yet within the protégé's reach, mentors will facilitate growth in these areas.

Finally, effective mentors also encourage the development of the whole person and the many facets of a scholarly professional identity. They take seriously their role in helping protégés build resilience, the ability to cope with significant challenges. Resilient individuals are realistic optimists who are committed to their work and adept at facing and solving problems. To build resilience in their protégés, mentors provide encouragement and emotional support, help protégés learn to reframe negative events, and aid them in cultivating effective coping strategies.

Wise mentors, like good teachers, treat errors as learning opportunities, using inquiry and dialogue to help protégés reflect on and learn from mistakes. For example, when an error stems from an inappropriate action, wise mentors might ask such questions as "What were you trying to accomplish in that situation?" or "What were you assuming when you chose to act in that way?" to help uncover faulty assumptions and ways of thinking.

Mentors play a critical role in fostering the growth and development of new faculty. In addition to helping protégés set goals for professional development, wise mentors are also attuned to their protégés' ongoing development as individuals and seek to foster growth that is holistic and enduring. Such mentors are adept at encouraging protégés to take on challenges that result in learning and development, whether the challenges are related to teaching, research, service, or other aspects of an academic career.

CHAPTER 8

Addressing Challenges and Obstacles

The development of a reflective diary can be a useful tool for mentors. By maintaining a diary, mentors can chart the progress of the relationship and the protege, record happenings of each meeting, identify positive and challenging situations, and find possible solutions to arising difficulties. It is common to find yourself off track in a conversation or the protege turning an academic problem into a personal issue. In having a record of the situation, the mentor can identify the cause of the drift and find an appropriate solution to rectify it. While the reflective diary should be an objective record of events, it also provides a chance for the mentor to vent their feelings on challenging situations. This method may be all that is needed for a mentor to overcome a challenging situation, but in the case that it isn't, the diary provides specific instances which can be brought to the mentor's supervisor for advice and guidance.

Experience has shown that mentoring, like any process, is not without its difficulties. There are several strategies mentors can employ to handle the expected and unexpected obstacles that may arise when working with a protege. One effective strategy is to anticipate possible challenges and discuss methods for handling them before the relationship begins. It is beneficial to engage in discussions that prepare the protege to understand the type of support that will be available. For example, a role-play conversation in which the mentor acts as if solving a problem and explains how a conversation of that nature might occur between the two of them. Mentors should share stories of when they have had difficulties and how they were able to overcome them. It is also helpful to discuss what the impact of the mentoring relationship has on a protege and how it may cause change or challenges for them in other areas of their life. While discussing these issues is not a fail-safe method for preventing obstacles, it can better equip the mentor and protege with the relative awareness and knowledge to overcome them.

CHAPTER 9

Celebrating Successes and Milestones

Celebrations at reaching a milestone need not come immediately. As Sheila continued to progress in her profession and integrate her teaching with critical reflection, she tackled and overcame many obstacles. These were not only learning experiences for her but inspirational stories for many other professional educators. She was able to talk to her peers about her experiences and move them to also employ the reflective teaching model after hearing how it had helped her through hard times. At the following staff meeting, I surprised Sheila with a short ceremony in front of her colleagues to commend her for professional growth. I presented her with a polished apple (reminiscent of the teacher's student) inscribed with her name and the words "reflective teacher and decision maker". The thoughtful applause she received helped her see that her personal journey had made a difference to others, and she was touched by their support. Celebrations can really reinforce that a good job has been done and often can provide added incentive to continue.

The concept of milestones permeates the landscape of our lives. Milestones signal change and passage - coming of age, graduation, marriage, and the birth of a first child - all are examples of milestones that call for celebration. Milestones also take place in the professional lives of educators, instructors, and mentors. When you and your protégé have reached a special point in your work together, celebrate it. This can be done with a card, an e-mail, a note or just some time together. These celebrations will help both of you in recognizing and remembering the accomplishments achieved. By celebrating the completion of the Comprehensive Exam of her Masters Degree with my student Michelle, we were able to take time to reflect on the hard work and emotional strain this milestone event involved. Recognizing her perseverance and dedication during this tough time was to later help bolster her resolve during a particularly rough time in her doctoral studies.

CHAPTER 10

Evaluating and Reflecting on the Mentorship

Once the evaluation process is complete, the mentor and protege should identify areas of strength and areas in which the mentorship could be improved. It is important to remember that both parties should not take anything as a failure, but rather a learning experience. After all, learning and growing is what mentoring is all about. The mentor should not take all the responsibility for areas of improvement, rather both parties need to find ways in which they can be equally involved in the process. A discussion should be had about what the future holds for the pair and how they can continue to grow. After identifying these areas, it is time for the mentor and the protege to redraft an informal mentorship agreement, with new goals for what they want to achieve in the remaining time that they have.

An excellent method to really understand the effectiveness of the mentorship is for the mentor and the protege to write a journal documenting their experiences and later swap journals and discuss what they had written. Sometimes things that are written in the journal are hard to express in the spoken word and both parties might gain a new perspective on the mentorship by doing this.

Another effective tool to evaluate the mentorship is to think back on significant events during the relationship and talk about how they helped the mentorship grow. These events can be anything from a childhood issue that showed while the protege was working with children, to a parenting situation that the mentor helped the protege through, to discussions about certain articles from the field. The more detailed they are in recollecting these events, the better the feel they will get for how the mentorship developed.

After a new mentor has completed the first few months of the mentorship, it is important for the mentor and the protege to evaluate and reflect on their relationship and the effectiveness of the mentorship. During the evaluation and reflection time, it is important that both the mentor and the protege be open-minded and honest with each other. Both parties should make a list of the goals they had for the mentorship and go through each one to evaluate if they were met. Chances are the goals will have changed since the beginning of the mentorship, however comparing it to what they originally thought will help demonstrate growth throughout the mentorship.

CHAPTER 11

Creating a Lasting Impact

Is the end of your relationship with the protege the end of the mentoring influence? Certainly, the legacy of a well-educated learner is a fine one. However, even when considering a limited relationship, the creation of a lasting positive educational impact is always a possibility. The mentor should always keep in mind the long-term goals and aspirations of their protege. Supporting these goals will increase the probability of a lasting influence. During the course of the relationship, the mentor can plant the seeds for future success and personal fulfillment in the protege, thereby continuing a positive impact long after the relationship has concluded. The mentoring relationship provides a safe place for the protege to take risks and try new directions. As the protege tries new endeavors, the mentor can help instill the ideal that one learns from success and failure and should always move forward. Encouraging a protege to view life as a series of developmental stages involving continuous self-reinvention provides a strategy for not merely surviving, but flourishing into old age. When a protege has reached this level of understanding, the mentor can be confident in a lasting positive impact.

CHAPTER 12

Conclusion

Using the bartender example again, I read an article discussing how the learner's needs should influence how we mentor. We also need to mentor the learner in a way that suits their needs. I realize this is true in the case of a learner needing to talk, but a bartender is often too busy or unaffordable to listen. The learner could seek another bartender who is able to listen or find another person, like a hairdresser, who will have more time to listen and talk. Either way, the learner influences the situation to best suit their needs. By keeping this in mind, the mentor can stay ready and flexible when the learner needs guidance. This can also prevent assignment errors by finding out first what the learner wants to do and why. If it doesn't align with the mentor's guidance paradigm, alternative solutions can be discussed.

Milton Keynes UK
Ingram Content Group UK Ltd.
UKHW031400011224
451790UK00009B/129